About the author

Julian Collins is an IT student currently living in Durham, North Carolina. Coming from an old military family, he was taught from a young age that the collective is more important than the individual. Due to health issues, however, he has never been able to serve in the military. But that has not stopped him from writing. Julian Collins received the John Foster West Scholarship in Poetry while attending Appalachian State University in 2011. In 2012, he attended Occupy Wall Street's September 17th protests alongside several other students from Appalachian State. Occupy was an international egalitarian movement that was highly critical of unbridled capitalism, corporate welfare, and American imperialism. The experience made a huge impression on Collins, as seeing so many people mobilized for revolutionary direct action made him long for even more auspicious undertakings. Julian Collins does not just write for himself; he writes for the nascent Revolution.

AS BELOW, SO ABOVE

JULIAN COLLINS

AS BELOW, SO ABOVE

Vanguard Press

VANGUARD PAPERBACK

A CIP catalogue record for this title is available from the British Library.

ISBN 978 1 80016 177 1

Vanguard Press is an imprint of Pegasus Elliot Mackenzie Publishers Ltd.
www.pegasuspublishers.com

First Published in 2021

Vanguard Press
Sheraton House Castle Park
Cambridge England

Printed & Bound in Great Britain

Dedication

I would like to dedicate my book to the revolutionaries of the past, present and future — for without their sacrifice there is no hope for humanity's deliverance from the genocidal evils of international finance capitalism.

Acknowledgements

I would like to acknowledge my mother, Lori Collins, for being that ever-present bulwark of unconditional love in my life, my father, Angel Cordero, for believing in my talent as an author and supporting me through the publication process, my sister, Rachel Cordero-Collins, for giving my life meaning. And my dog, Schatzie, for giving my life joy. I would also like to acknowledge Stephen Badras for editing *As Below, So Above* in its formative stages.

Contents

Contraband (Ode to Charon)

Ferryman,
I ain't no stowaway,
drown me my soul to stray,
that I might know the day.

Can't you see!

I'm your zealotry,
your hallow shine,
your entropy,
your borderline!

Your apathy,
your serpentine,
your gravity,
your paradigm!

Ferryman!
Are you the Nyx?
Are you the Acheron?
Are you the Styx?

Are you the river?
Are you the path?
Are you the giver?
Are you the wrath?

Contraband,
you ain't no stowaway,
drown you your soul to stray,
that you might know the day.

Can't you see!

You're my zealotry,
my hallow shine,
my entropy,
my borderline!

My apathy,
my serpentine,
my gravity,
my paradigm!

Contraband!
Are you a loner?
Are you a goner?
Are you a stoner?

Are you lost?
Are you found?
Are you frost?
Are you drowned?

Ferryman,
I ain’t no stowaway,
drown me my soul to stray,
that I might know the day.

Can’t you see!

I’m your contraband,
your tragedy,
your poker hand,
your strategy!

Your firebrand,
your cavalry,
your motherland,
your apogee!

Contraband,
you ain’t no stowaway.
drown me your soul to stray,
that you might know the day.

Can’t you see!

You’re my contraband,
my tragedy,
my poker hand,
my strategy!

My firebrand,
my cavalry,
my motherland,
my apogee!

Witness

Hades, hearken to me.

Fell gods of the abyss,
witness a civilian's sophistry.
Waters of the River Styx,
witness a citizen's poetry.
Charon, sons of Dis,
witness a guardian's eternity.

Witness me, my mothers,
my fathers,
my sisters,
my brothers.

Witness me, my opaque heart,
witness me, my initiated mystery.

Witness me, my body,
witness me, my soul,
witness me, my country,
witness me, my whole.

Witness me, my Heathens,
witness me, my apostates,
witness me, my reasons,
witness me, my Fates.

Witness me, my flowers,
witness me, my love,
witness me, my powers,
witness me, my dove.

Witness me, Lucretia,
tell me you hate me so,
hate me for my wrath,
but love me for my bow.

Witness me, Dulcinea,
tell me you love me so,
love me for my fury,
but hate me for my flow.

Witness me, my black rose,
chase me across time,
chase me across your clothes,
chase me across the rhyme.

I give myself to Hades,
I give myself to the Styx,
I give myself to Charon,
I give myself to the sons of Dis.

Without condition,
without sanction;

without a home,
without a nation.

Without a price,
without a toll;
without a body,
without a soul.

My Blood

My blood courses a hollow counting
through my fickle veins,
capricious capillaries
that pump copperish cells
from ventricle to muscle,
from aorta to artery,
from organ to spinal column
through fleshy causeways haunted
with methodical memories.

Through hallowed halls that echo entropic
with ancestral instinct,
walls covered in a cardiac calligraphy
that spells the name
but paints the portrait.

There are eons in those paintings,
ages in those mosaics that,
cubit by cubit,
measure Michelangelo mystical
and Machiavelli mammalian.

There are civilizations on that canvas,
temples rendered rubble,
ruins rendered cathedral
by a painter's hand burdened

with brush
and palette.

Dancing the stroke and riposte
unrepentant across the murals,
splattering the colors in an ascetic haze
that rings alarm and sings lullaby.

My blood is a fallout shelter
that moonlights as an art exhibit,
pumping breathable oxygen through the vents
like the air conditioning at a Broadway brothel
where starving artists choose between food and
sex.

My heart beats loath and cold my blood
through sullen limbs
that limp the cripple's misery
and dance the squatter's ecstasy.

My heart is a crude war drum
that heralds my Blood from
beat to beat,
measure to measure,
verse to verse
and beyond ballistic baryonics bouncing off of
boarded boats all flashing lights and fleeting
Blood Feuds bridging baptism by forlorn hope;

gravitational confirmation by abyssal falling to fatalistic rebirth enveloped in an electronic darkness that Sparks luminous shadows of the mute nocturnal vacuum.

My Blood hemorrhages sullen
the Long Count interred
in a metallic shrine
to Lost Children;
scornful and sighing,
heaving and hurting.

My blood is the seafloor
that purifies the water
cell by cell
in an opaque
paraconsistent procession
of breathless bubbles
and binding.

My blood is that bathos atmospheric
that gravity pulls to her bosom
in an embrace maternal of
sullen sinking.

My Blood is the empty chairs,
the empty tables that
attend absent communion

in an empty temple
to lost loves and
unrequited causes.

Invocation of Athena

Broken grandfather clocks
toll the bell of the disgraced Goddess
holding aloft a Flame that She is
ashamed to peer through.
She pretends that she doesn't know
what Uncle Sam does to her daughter,
her nephew,
the nuns,
the choir boys.
The half staff that swan songs
a collaterally damaged record.
Unwritten,
Unspoken,
Unsung soliloquy in Her Heart,
too Opaque for condition.
Too soothspoke for recess.
but so… Elegant
in her Ignominy Sacred.
Hallowing the holy fields
where killer angels
pejorative legitimate targets
painted as ascendant
chameleon lasers that
savor the sport and hunt
the apostate.

Oh, Liberty.
Witness me, Liberty.
witness me.

Taste me your own Grace,
drink me your own Beauty,
dine me your own
deathless doorbells that
ordain your Destiny.
Rewind me your alarm clock
cacophonous the tortured
exile you dance as shots of
cranberry cognac.
Take me back your womb,
your objectively permanent adolescence,
your sensorimotor peek-a-boo,
your pre-operational proselytizing.
Your concrete copper calves
that Stand as a testament
to your consecrated constitution.
Your formal courtship that you're
too polite to ask for.
Your terminal mosh pit that
the system's too fragile to frolic in
as the purple haze pedestal
on which tempted trophies are
attached is shaken through
porous walls that fall the stimulated

poverty your heretics institutionalize.
Give me your Heart.
Your tired,
your poor,
your huddled masses.
Breathe me free your wretched
refuse of these, your teeming shores.
Shoulder me faithfully,
knee me the nonbeliever,
headbutt me the heretic,
frown through me as you
jab and kill.
Parry me, my hands
loath and cold,
sullen.
Let us sleep now.

Catatonic catacombs echo the bones
upon which are inscribed the absolute truth.
Root for the celebrity,
but salute the enemy.
March in formation,
but demand recitation
of the Omertà sworn in secrecy
but peripherally peer reviewed.
Allude to the axiom
you pretend not to know.

The autonomous interlude of
neo-Newtonian ideological operation
snorts the processed bones of
peculiar pests just before the next bound.
Surgical in your solemn surrender…
or lack thereof.
Under and before the call of duty
the temperature is measured in Fahrenheit,
Celsius and Kelvin as coded crypts
listen in on words I never said.
Dread the Monet paintings you pretend to admire.
Mask me your message unmemorized
and interrogated from this shell.

Oh, Belle, would you be mine?

Propose her your prophecies
too persistent to be permitted.
Burn these shadows
in your order antecedent.
No precedent,
no precipitation,
no poisoned chalice of malice
as moist as the choice between cold causeways
and diving headfirst into oceans of fire
that Parisian choirs seditiously praise
through invisible curtains that
click, roar and catcall.

The Sacred Feminine beaten,
dragged and raped through
the electronic ticking and tocking
of the global clock.
No knock,
no glock,
no warrant,
No more wanting:
just Desire.
It does not matter how tired you are!
It does not matter how happy you are!
It does not matter how split-second
temporal registry hangs heads,
streets, whole cities as lowly as squatter's rights.
Rage with the undying of the night!
Biological corruption opens, closes
and reopens the local zoo as any
local patrons are sent to Coventry,
brigands and broads both.

Broadway is dark tonight.
Luminous,
Nocturnal,
Blinding,
Binding the love of a country
that made man and woman both
from a spear, a rib, a spinal column,

an extraterrestrial gesticulation of the primal prowess
that unmasks only the worthy,
only the mute,
only the chosen.
The love of colony
that made xenophilic acidic ants
hiss the Prison of Nantes interstellar
to impregnated sacrifices to the Tao
without quid pro quo through corridors
that echo evanescent the celestial void.
The phantom pains that coincide with each
ride or die chorus, verse, and bridge
over-encumbered with fleeing burghers
that murder each other when the street
is overburdened with toxicity,
forgotten as military necessity.
Recalled as a suburban deluge of mini-mall
sanctuaries barricaded as bayoneted zipliners
get up with the sickness.

Oh, Mystery.
Witness me, Mystery.
witness me.

Phallic imagery triggers telepathic static
across the relative infrastructure
of Westphalian incest gone internecine.

The Feminine Chalice lures the child molesters,
the rapists, the school shooters
into autonomous sensory meridian response
echolocation that drops dimes, quarters and halves
as quickly as it's typed.
Staff the tranquility of the transferent
reincarnation
that Beethoven's Danse Macabre
dragon king tunes may codify ancient voices
into solitaire sonatas that bonsoir
only the most callous of hearts
Good luck and good night.

Architecture tactfully crafted
as lullabies are sung to sleeping samurai
whose shogun naps off the temporal taxation
as a hissing lotus interred in the sensory
deprivation
of the Sacrificial Temptation of the Void.
Awake, asleep, fleet as the silent run
that sung to the hunters,
killers and banana boats alike
who were revoked of their SOS
in the name of command responsibility:
the one true standard of officership.
You will follow your orders or
your orders will follow you.
Find you,

drink you as Code Red Mountain Dew
for the cover you blew.
The skin you shed,
the stale bread you
washed down with poor mead.
Greed is not good:
welcome to the choke point.
No fences,
no sixpence,
no pseudoscientific irreverence
of zombie doctors who stumbled
over armed collegiate barricades that
stood, stand and will stand tall…
even if they fell, fall or will fall.
The day they get you is gone, boy.
and you're gone with it.

Winding through the claustrophobic
cyclone of unrecalled carnage.
The muzzle flashes,
the cordite,
the smoke
that consumed the metropolis
as slow dancers in a burning room
that replicate to beacons of Liberty,
Justice and Sovereignty.
Dope pumps through the veins
of those that mansplain the lesbian

difference between chauvinist pedophilia
and Greco-Roman sexual knowledge of Confucian
Self,
Virtue, and Guardianship of the Polis.
Go cry about it,
why don't you?
We're here to hurt you,
hearse you,
worse you.
Immerse you in tongues that
you don't know you can speak.
Utter any word save for mercy,
defeat, repeat.

Witness me;
Her Voice that Speaks as running for re-ignition
of the ancient Flame that Consumed by
urban inferno whole city-states, countries,
empires.

Sires and Madams,
scream Her Name
as they pluck your angel wings
feather by feather,
laughter Her Letters as they
seek your flesh by feeding frenzy,
smile Her Similitude as she Sings
your excruciating lullaby

as a collectively unconscious Whisper
the Fidelity of which is real, authentic, true:
whether you believe it or not.

We don't die,
we multiply.
We don't lie,
we amplify.
We don't why,
we grimace.
We don't testify,
we witness.

Oh, Athena.
Witness me, Athena.
witness me.

Colony

Colony, Colony, Colony;
Colony, Colony, Colony.

The Colony is calling me.
Calling me,
calling me.

As six insectoid legs propel me through the grass
while the Red Queen's antennae vibrate from
subterranean sanctuary in a language only us fire
ants can comprehend.

"Help!
We're under attack!
Worker ants!
Soldier Ants!
Now is the time to fight back!
Report to the Colony, stat!"

The Colony,
the Colony,
the Colony has called on me.
Called on me,
called on me.

We chant as we rush to the one gate the termite advance could not overwhelm for our only chance was for the Foragers to rally round the Queen as if we were living in a dream but dying in real life.

That woodpecking Scum met our surge as the baby larvae observed through their infantile feelers the horrors of dismembered Soldier ants shaking in claustrophobic death throes while their mandibles snapped a Spartan roar.

The worker ants all sallied forth so us Soldiers could make it to the keep like hundreds of white rabbits running down a pack of hunters singing the song of angry ants.

Will you join in our parade?
Will you be strong and stand with me?
Beyond the lemonade is there a world you long to see?

While we died from torn antenna to ripped abdomen and beyond chamber-to-chamber melees melting acidic martyrdoms as the weaker Workers rushed the larvae to the Red Queen's holdfast within the keep trying their best to ignore the Empty Chairs and Empty Tables they could feel clearing just a few causeways above.

Colony,
Colony,
Colony.

The Colony is mauling me,
mauling me,
mauling me.

As a few of the Red Queen's maids even tore off their feelers as not to hear the horrors of evolutionary combat, preferring life as a deaf mute to hearing their kin refuse triage as the workers and the soldiers fall back to the keep, pawning their lives dearly as they scream the howl of dying ants.

For Queen and Colony,
for Queen and Colony,
for.

Collapsed antechambers as we
rallied round the Red Queen,
admittedly quivering in fear
at the thought
of the loss
of the larvae
who were too numerous to deny the termite horde
their treasured feast.

The Red Queen
angrily
snapped her mandibles
at her birthing sack,
ordering it to be
severed
that she may die a good death.

Clicking her mandibles
and screaming her antennae
such that there was yet one
ant in the colony that still
roared "Death. Death; Death!"

She took her place in front of the soldiers,
workers, maids and larvae, sucking in one
of her last breaths.

"Colony, Colony; Colony,
The Colony has called on We,
Called on We,
Called on We."

She sung to the fallen subterranean fortress
as six limbed exoskeletons
steeled themselves against
certain death, antennae ceased quivering and

mandibles bit with disciplined precision.
As the termites began to break through the
collapsed entrance to
the Royal Chamber the Red Queen
laughed at her fortune
to die such a good death,
drawing her last breath and
declaring in a triumphant vibration,
shaking as she does it before
waiting for herself to settle down.

"Comrades,
if we must die,
then we all die Together.
If we all die Together
then they can never
take that away
from Us!"

Colony, Colony, Colony;
Colony, Colony, Colony.

For We and Colony;
For We and Colony.

Athena Herself

Ha-ha;
ha-ha-ha-ha-ha,
what a foolish mortal.

To think that he could ever speak for Me.

The flawless blonde beauty of the ancient
Athenian phalanx
who teased her fellow hoplites into throwing their
lives away
as unworthy suitors who could never
soothe these loins or speak our Tongue.

Oh, he would deign speak my lips.
But would he taste my lisp,
hear my words on a wisp of the breeze
that bends trees, knees, and enemies
till they break as a mortal string
the Fates happened to scissor?

Would he trigger my Path
and incur the wrath of my jealous sisters,
suitors, and other extramarital relations?

He says nothing, preferring my Omerta to
enunciated speech,

For he knows how he would perform in the breach
from the first blood to the last stand and beyond
postmodern shootouts from street-to-street
routs to besieged redoubts shelled into
the lack thereof submission.

Unbowed, unbent, unknown as the Name
of the Last Zealot of Masada who put the Tribe
before their very soul that every believer would
know
that damnation is a better fate than defeat.

Lo;
Lo, find me.
Lo, find me where the women
will mince the meat.
Lo, find me where the men will not retreat.
Lo, find me where the people truly take the street.

Ha-ha;
ha-ha-ha-ha-ha,
what a foolish mortal.

Providing a portal to my feats of
martial glory as the
storied warrior princess of Athens, laughing as
I stab and slash at Spartan hoplites who were
aghast at being slaughtered by a daughter

who bore no sons but stole many
mothers' offspring.

Ha-ha;
Ha-ha-ha-ha-ha.

Especially the fools who thought that
this thot could be slayed by a sling
and a stone.
I am Athena,
I am Rome.
I am the celestial abyss into which you plunge
as a talking yellow sponge, an aquamarine fish,
or a red herring.

I am at Home
on the field and do not know how to yield,
how to surrender, how to render
onto pretenders any honor
they did not earn.

If you can teach Us otherwise, then come and try
my spear, my shield, my armor, or my toga
for you will never be worthy of a yoga session by
my
side as I only fornicate with the ride-or-die
soldiers of the International Proletarian
Revolution

whose elocutions advocate the virtues of the
Ancient Greek city-state.

Rape me if you dare,
date me if you're rare.
Dare to breathe my air
if you are in earshot
for you must have forgot
My motherfucking Name.

I am the Spear,
I am the Shield,
I am the Fear,
I am the Field.

I am Athens,
I am Rome,
I am Greece,
I am Om.

I am not Athena.

She died defending the Acropolis from Spartan
hordes
as when Her spear shattered, She drew Her sword
and cut down as many crimson-cloaked
cataphracts
as She could.

For she was forced from her own phalanx
over her Moon's Blood offending
a jealous suitor or two.
Or three Spartan samurai felled by My sword
as when I died without a word, laughing
at their expense while my taut, captive
throat was Sliced into a Socratic smile.

Ha-ha;
ha-ha-ha-ha-ha.

Lo, I am not Athena,
the Omerta incarnate,
The flawless blonde hyena of the ancient Athenian
phalanx who teased her fellow hoplites into
throwing their lives away as unworthy suitors who
could never soothe these loins or speak our
Tongue.

Who traded a fleeting
life for one eternal.
What a foolish mortal.
To think that he could
never speak for Me.

Fidelity
is not to seem,

it is to be.
Ha-ha;
ha-ha-ha-ha-ha.

Ode to Neptune

Oh, Neptune,
I'm drowning…
are you?

I can't tell if this ocean is blue,
purple or green
but I won't gargle,
I won't scream.

The closed hatch
that would mean
the breathlessness
is becoming,
rather than to seem.

Or seeming,
rather than to become,
oh Neptune!

I don't falter,
I don't run,
I've no son for my name
but I've got a poem!
I've got a claim!
I've got my aimless artistry!
Hearken to me,

Neptune!
For my Ship
is no broken home!

I don't backbite,
I don't recall,
it is but a small courtesy
that I do you, Neptune.

Do me a smaller favor,
for I would savor an Ocean,
I would savor a sweet,
I would savor a potion,
I would even savor defeat.

I'm drowning in this
decadence, Neptune.
But have you already succumbed
to these scorned seas?
Are you in need of resuscitation?
From these oceans
of that avarice
that drives the homeless
from hearth and home.

Where would I roam without
these nets that have
ensnared me as bulla men.

Oh Neptune,
did the Sun bear witness
to your drowning beneath
the same liquidity that would
bury me?

Did the other Gods watch?
And laugh in vanity,
as you succumbed to a sea
you once swore to defend?

Oh, Neptune,
I'll never hear the end of it.
But hear me,
star-struck wanderer
of the Seven Seas.

All I do is seem…
but one day,
oh Neptune,
would that I could be!

Would that I could walk the deck
of an unbroken Home!
Would that I could see an ocean
as the most fertile loam!

For Neptune,

this decadence…
is all that I have known,
all that I have been.
The closed hatch
that would mean
the breathlessness
is becoming,
rather than to seem.
Being,
rather than to dream.

Road to Neptune

I was not born a sailor,
Neptune,
as you were born
a body celestial.

I was born to a bloody,
powdery river, Neptune…
were that I was born
to the Styx instead.

All my good intentions
have fled, Neptune…
have yours, too, fled
from hearth and home?

I'll tread your road, Neptune,
I'll tack your trajectory,
I'll even roar your name,
Neptune!

Who else would I have to blame?
Neptune!
Who else would have such claim?
Neptune!
Is my poetry too tame?
Neptune!

Have my oceans passed me on by?
As a bottled message to a dead God,
who forgot to read my words of praise?
All drunk on the drowned waters
of middling poets whose couplets
just weren't good enough.

Whose still waters
just didn't run deep enough.
Whose silence
Just wasn't quiet enough.
Whose letters
just weren't sad enough.
Whose trust
just wasn't fragile enough.

Am I fragile enough
for you now, Neptune?
For your road calls to me
from the mute vacuum of space
to the surging depths of the sea,
for I don't just want to seem, Neptune…
I want to be!

I want to breathe deep the frigid stillness
of stellar oceans that stand on celestial
ceremony all silent stars and roaring

abysses that are darker than even my
heart of hearts for my art must not be good
enough
for distant fathoms that even sailors fear to
invoke.

I'll tread your road, Neptune.
I'll tack your constellation…
for I am a patient believer in
reincarnation and all you've got is time.

Code to Neptune

Call me a heretic
if you dare
for the ocean is deeper
than how much you care.

Call me a loser
if you just seem
for the seas see through
this nightmarish Dream.

Call me a monster
if you would misunderstand
these words that would deliver me
from this forsaken land.

Call yourself reprobate,
if you would condone
that avariciousness that
spurns hearth and home.

Am I droning, Neptune?
Do you pardon my licentiousness?
For my Country is moaning, Neptune.
Is She beyond your forgiveness?

Do not loathe me for my loquaciousness,

or love me for my lyricism,
but guide me through this viciousness,
that I might learn asceticism.

Hear me in your depths
as intently as I long
for that deep that liberates,
that current made of song.

Heed me, Neptune,
for this is no idle prayer,
and the waters may liberate
just as much as the air.

Do you know me, Neptune?
Or am I still a stranger,
lost to this avarice,
that curls my fists in anger.

Are you angry, Neptune?
That no virtue commands
the seas,
the skies,
the abyss,
the stars.
Am I best beseeching you,
or Mars?

Are you impotent, Neptune?
Do you no longer command
the fortune of the fleets
due to supply and demand.

Are you a lost cause, Neptune?
Are my words futile?
For I long to sail
from the Azores to the Nile.

From Venus to Pluto,
and beyond the horizon's reach,
from Mars' mountains,
to some distant beach.

Perhaps you don't hear me, Neptune,
perhaps my words are all in vain,
maybe you are a lost cause,
maybe you are worth the pain.

Ferryman

I've forgotten more beautiful poetry
than I'd care to remember.
Can't tell if my heart rests on ice
or a bed of embers.

Can't tell if the old gods listen
and ignore or
if I'm just sore from a life spent
listless and waiting.

Debating within my self of selves
whether reality is this surface
or the depths beneath,
not bequeathed the truth
but a lightning bolt
that shook the roof
when I sung through my tooth
that song that tingled and seared.

Maybe the old gods did hear,
that desperate, forgotten song
that roared all wrong with the world,
beyond a reckless abandon.

Should they respond, as they did before,
may their well wishes take me to a distant shore,

where the core of my being might take root,
and thick branches might offshoot from my frame.

I don't need the world to remember my name,
but this apostasy, this shame, this blameless
innocence that spends the years,
fears not this avarice but tears.

And tumultuous drags us towards
that midnight clock,
where even the static dies out and this flock
follows our bad shepherds to that cliff,
adrift amongst the rocks and contraband.

Bones shattered and wool unsheared,
of what use was that fear of public speaking
that led us here?

Of what use were the rules
that brought us to our doom?
Our shepherds are but fools
that convince us the tomb is a womb.

So I sang to Charon,
I sang to Hades,
I sang to Athena,
and Neptune too.

I sang for living and the dead,
for the giving and the dread,
for the Fates and the Thread,
for the gates and the tread.

For the God that watches us suffer,
and allows such evil to persist,
I thought that I might be a buffer,
I thought my soul would not exist.

Do you hear me now, Ferryman?
I've forgotten your song completely!
Do you fear me now, Ferryman?
I dedicate my song to Phillis Wheatley!

Hear me now, Ferryman!
For she is my muse and my standard.
Fear me now, Ferryman!
For she is my blues and my vanguard!

Not Waterloo

As the two armies marched at each other
all tipping flags, stoic shaking, and horses chewing,
a Young Second Lieutenant noticed a glimmer
to the right of the formation beneath a line of trees.

His Not General happened
upon him then, having just
ordered a countermarch as to confront it.

"You saw it then, didn't you?"
remarked the seasoned
general of men as he continued,
"The Danse Macabre?"

The Second Lieutenant says, shakily, "The Danse Macabre?"
"I couldn't believe it when I first saw it either;
burly Jamaican men, invisible, dreadlocked, clicking like
the Masai and just as talented with a spear."

The Second Lieutenant gulped twice,
shook his head in
an ancient anger as his general recounted to him

how the Danse Macabre
would slice through ranks of
redcoat regulars.

Clicking the language of the
Congo as they
chopped
the dread Danse of the Jamaican tribal
warriors, invisible as they do it.

"Do you believe in God, Ser?"
asked the Uppity Second Lieutenant.

"No," replied Not Cornwallis,
"Not since I first witnessed
the Jamaican Gods of Death
mow us down as the Japanese
bladed spear monks with bolts
of blue lightening and judo throws."

"Is it an enemy to us, Ser?"
The suddenly steely Second
Lieutenant asked his most
superior Officer.

"If by 'enemy'
you mean we are
their prey to be hunted;

I've ordered a countermarch
to confront them."

The uppity second lieutenant then asked
"Since there's four
of them…
may I lead a
party of three
other forlorns
against the Dance
Macabre?"

Who he could observe hanging skinless
bodies from trees both exposed and hidden In
plain sight as both armies seemed not to
notice or react to the grizzly scene while these.

Afro-Jamaican Voodoo Gods of War
casually hang up the coats of their prey.

"Sure, my son, yourself and three other
fools with no House to inherit the honor
of that would sooner be grown into the
grass here on the field of.

'Not Waterloo.'

Than face the
infinite lash of the withering
sands of time, the only means of transcending
them being feats
of martial
Glory."

The dread stories of Nelson's victory at
Trafalgar bounced round the
Uppity Second Lieutenant's
mind as he drunkenly said "Sure, m'lord" to his
General while wondering
whether or not those dreadlocked squatters of the
Dance Macabre didn't slay the
Way for Horatio Nelson's fire ships… or lend a
spear or three to Leonidas at Thermopylae.

Or;
Five
to Caesar at Alesia
who fought on all fronts
while the Gods themselves
Held off the enemies of Rome.

The Uppity Second Lieutenant takes a deep
breath before dashing back to camp – the promise
of entrance into a noble House making his
fangs flare,

snarl,
and
tremble.

So he arrived at his mates' outdoor campfire
but eyebrows were raised, smirks wrinkled,
and kits were prepared as the Four Second
Lieutenants assembled at the rear of the right
flank while the British Army wheeled to
accommodate
their illegal tride.

The Four Would-be Generals looked down the
field at the Danse Macabre while the infantrymen,
artillerists and cavalry began
to notice the invisible,
dreadlocked Jamaican Gods
of clicking Masai Death
hanging the flayed corpses of English
and French men alike.

When Not Cornwallis tipped
his hat at the Four Second Lieutenants
of Not Waterloo, they all drew their rapiers,
with which they had spent
countless hours practicing their
fencing, and began a slow trot towards

the shade in which resided
the Danse Macabre.

The Danse Macabre were busy hanging
flayed corpses when the
Uppity Second Lieutenant
shouted "En Macabre!" at the top of his allegedly
frail lungs,
drawing and raising his rapier
such that the glint
would register in the
Eyes of the marching band.

The Forlorn Four Second
Lieutenants, wraithlike, drew
their blades and held them straight
into the air as the marching band began to
play the Danse Macabre, that dreadful tone that
paralyzes enemies
for pennies, pounds, or
sixpence.

The Jamaican
or Masai or African
or Japanese Gods of Death
Started
a slow, deliberate
march at the uppity British officers

who were shocked to see their rapid advance
reciprocated by an almost dancing
squat-step in rhythm
with the
British marching band
as
Not Cornwallis
remarked that he had
never seen belles' hair turn
in such unison as the
Danse Macabre.

The Forlorn Four
slowed the pace for a breath
or two, made uneasy at the sight of
the Macabre decloaking defiantly and angrily
shaking their dreads till Not Cornwallis roared
"Are you
redcoats or empty
Saddles?"
and Fired his pistol
in the air above their heads.

With that,
the Uppity Lieutenant
Tore after the Danse Macabre,
sheathing his sword as he came withing shooting

distance and drew his flintlock pistol, giving his
comrades
time to sheathe and draw
before he shouted
"Fire!"

Discarding their spent pistols
as to draw their swords
in time to tilt as fencing flintlock
knights with the dreaded
extraterrestrial menace of the
30 Years' War that mowed
down the troops of colonial
nations as the Egyptian
Death Gods of the Patois.

Their shots wounded one of the death gods,
as the thousands of Redcoats
finally witnessed that
the Dance Macabre could bleed, cheering on
the Four Forlorn Knights as "Huzzah!"

"Huzzah, Huzzah!"

The Uppity Second Lieutenant forgot to say
a prayer as he charged into
what was never there, dancing the Macabre as

both armies watched the unwinnable fight the
Forlorn Four had picked.

The redcoat Actual General ordered
his refusing mortars to fire
on the scene of the melee when
only the Uppity Lieutenant had joined battle after
tilting with a Shinigami, scoring a neckshot
to resounding huzzahs as the alleged welp's
Horse was tackled to the grassy
field to the neighs of his
Mount.
And the death
throes of the
Rider.

For he, to His own shock,
pierced one of the Gods'
necks with his fencing blade,
roaring as the angered
Dansers surrounded
him and cut him
down.

Smiling,
for the dreadlocked foe he fell
was Laughing at his fortunate fate
to die so well.

"I swear
I never
meant to
order him
in there.
Where they slashed and
thrust and rolled through
four of them at once and grunted
as they punched one to the very ground
and both armies let out a roar of "Huzzah!
Huzzah, Huzzah!" when as one was slain by a
saber
mounted cavalier that inspired the deer that were
the entire Cavalry of France who
half shit their pants,
half gawked at the unordered
sight of Not Cornwallis' Gents
who were worth their sixpence
and more after they slaid the Danse
Macabre when they failed to detonate their inferno
that would have dragged
them all to hell as the Greco-Roman Gods
themselves battled with the orphaned
infantry who were as Forlorn as their Traitorous
charge laid bare the true Gentleman
in charge of the military band that hummed and
hissed and shelled the Macabre Danse

into the tempo of a rolling fencing match against
hunters your average human being would
not stand a chance of besting as no Olympic
fencing will prepare you for a true ballet recital
which that Danse Macabre surely Learned.

"En Macabre."
Quoth Not Cornwallis
as he sips a stout glass
of only the purest sherry,
"En Macabre."

Forlorn Hope

The Halls were livid,
the Ancient Walls were quaking;
such a Forlorn Hope.

They fell one by one,
grimacing of the Long Count;
taut with such Sorrow.

The Throne Room was still,
the guards were just a deluge;
the Hope was just One.

Roaring the Good Blood,
anachronistic Zealot;
a Spear and a throw.

The Kill of the Age,
the wounded Detonation;
the Best of the Blood.

Lady Liberty

Staring into the East,
I can see you stumbling back to me.
The stench of oil on your breath like liquor,
blood money lines your pockets like lint.
Terror color codes hang from your eyelids
the same way nooses hung from trees.

Watch the bodies ebb and flow
as they sway in the breeze.
Arms tatted up with childhood images of your
American dreams but
your body has become a nightmare.

What happened to you?
You used to love me
you used to say my name like I was your sun,
your stars,
your sky,
your reason why;
you used to call me your Lady.
But now I'm just Liberty.
And you say my name like
you own me but I don't own you.

Say my name like you used to.
Say it like my words till ring true

through your ears like a proverb.
Give me your tired,
your poor,
your huddled masses
yearning to be free.
Give me your heart.

Pull your hands from the levers of the machine
and push them through your rib cage like
protesters pushing through riot shields.
Push through your ribs like
you pushed into the West.
Pushing aside the bars of your cage like
tribes
and every time a bone clatters
on the floor another culture dies.

Brittle bits of calcium scattered
without reservation.
Push through those lungs
that heave like train pistons:
a thousand streams of steam
erupting from your mouth.

And with both hands
pushing through your chest
maybe you could feel your heartbeat.
As slow as a slave's speech

and as strong as a slave's shoulders!
As rapid as a politician's lies
and as sincere as their eyes!
Your heart is a holding cell!
Where you keep everything
you don't want me to see!

Shoved into secret places
as dark as my shadows.
Plainly written in history books
in schools that can't afford to fix the lights.
But as the sun rises in the East it blinds me
The same way you blinded me with your walk,
your stride,
your eyes:
dark like black holes
and radiant like suns.

I knew you would do for me what no others could;
and as my dull copper turned green with the ocean breeze
I could hear love songs
in the waves crashing
against the shoreline.

But now you seem to think that…
you're the best I can do.
Like you're the only one that can

pluck these heartstrings.
You think I'm yours because I
stand on your shores but
I am not my body.
This green-tinged copper skin is a hollow shell!
What shape could capture the embodiment of
freedom?
And what you think you ain't got competition?

I've got revolutionaries
courting me at every nook and cranny!
Dying to feel the touch of my skin!
Do you not know
how many martyrs
died
to read my holy books?
To what darkness
they plunged
to see my light!
They would gouge out their eyes
to hear me speak!
Bleed from both hands and feet
nailed to two two-by-fours
for my kiss on their cheek
and you think
you're better than me?

My eyes face East

but I see
everything!
I peer through your thorns
and see the dead rose inside!

The withered bits of red flesh:
all that's left of your heart!
Your life!
You are a star-spangled skeleton
dancing on a lie.

Dancing on the soldier's box
to those twenty-one shots,
dancing on the burial grounds
your fathers bled for,
dancing in fields of green that
you burned to a crisp,
dancing till the vinyl disc burns
and the turntable crumbles,
dancing till you need me to lift
your battered body from the floor.

And maybe…
I will…
and maybe I will leave you heartbroken.
For the miles you took
with the inches I gave
and maybe…

you will set things straight.
Before that
dance floor
becomes your grave.

Athena

"Out of the Phalanx,"
while Sacred Athens burned Red;
"You are on your Moon."

The People Sobbing,
yet somehow, She was "Mooning;"
"Omertá, Cowards."

The Spartans all Reeled,
as Athena Broke their Ranks;
as She Slashed and Killed.

She Bled them Weeping,
She Bled the Acropolis;
"Gods, what have we done."

The Hoplités Wept,
then the Cowards ran away;
pulling out their Hair.

Kamikaze

I wrote her a love poem
and put it in my chest pocket.
Maybe it'll burn through my ribs
and latch itself to my heart.
Maybe if I plummet into the sea
it would plummet with me
and I could relive the edges
of her body with lines of poetry.
Maybe those bullets
would break
through the cockpit sending shells
streaming through my body like
rays of the rising sun,
shards of
poetry and glass
putting me to sleep in the sky.

They called us Kamikaze.
"Divine winds" but there's a contradiction,
divine winds do not die.
But I…
I fail to see the divinity in packing
planes full of explosives and
plowing them into enemy ships.
I never thought…
I never thought that I…

would meet Americans like this:
sitting in this cockpit with their rounds
reaching up at me riddling my metal coffin.
Poem to my chest,
hands on the stick.
I stuck
to the course,
pushing it
down, down, down.
I fell…
I fell like a treacherous angel
into the depths of hell,
that burning lake of fire below me,
flashes and streaks like lightning bolts
rising up from the sea.

And I could see
my comrades turn to burning metallic shreds
around me…
their wings ripped away;
she said
it was suicide.
"But honey, is it suicide if you are samurai,"
If you are choosing to die…
"Is it suicide if you believe?"
If you can see their eyes looking up at you
as clearly as the veins of autumn leaves.

Plummeting to put an end to you,
to us,
to me.
A bullet
rips through the glass.
My face,
it stings.
I cling
to the stick,
every second
was a decade
as the deck of the battleship grew bigger
the wings of my plane screamed
at the prospect
of their self-destruction.

"Do not die for nothing!" she said.

"No, I will die for everything," I said.
"For our dignity,
our culture,
our history.
Because like it or not
It's them or us and I will never
let them touch you."
It's not enough just to say it! I have to reiterate it
in every revolution of the propeller blades pulling
me towards eternity!

They could see…
They could see that rising sun rag
wrapped around my head:
a neatly tied bandana of white
and red.
They could see me
through those gun sights and flashes
but could they see their lover's eyes the way I see
yours?
Death is opening the door,
they couldn't put me down
and I can see it now.
An explosion of fire,
metal pressed plane parts
and a poem:
burnt into my heart.
And honey,
I never thought I would meet Americans like this.

The Yell of Furies

The Bulls were Running,
along with the young, eager;
no swan songs were heard.

There he rode, Stony,
a peculiar Hand aloft;
to such Feigned envy.

Between the Present,
but between the Precision;
Lo, between the Fire.

A stunned Silence,
a Smirk and a Mute neighing;
the Yell of Furies.

Their eyes wide: disbelief,
Lo, they took the Bayonet;
'Twas not theirs to Give.

The Catacombs of Paris

For ossuary atrophy
stumbling from atrium
to causeway and back.

Lost to the lonely tunnels,
howling a sobbing
swan song all batteries,
backpacks and broken bones.
Tripping from tactile tomb
to cavernous crypt.

Blinded by tears and mucus,
screaming themselves hoarse
at the whispering shadows
in a hopeless hostel to
the dearly departed,
condemned and damned.

Panicked in the plunge,
trapped in the tortuous void
of the hesitant and
impressionable.

For catastrophes unrequited
that send futile signals
from subterranean sanctum,

electronic death amidst
collapse in fetal agony,
weeping the song of
angry men.

Crawling
from Macabre mausoleum
to halls of horrors
that gaze and walk
but do not pursue.

For despondent wallowing,
tear ducts emptied of
the hope those eyes
descended into the abyss with,
hollow, desolate, doomed.

Cradled in darkness,
callous to the cruelty
of coffin chorales
that echo ethereal
but measure Miserable.

Disconnected in the deathless
depths of derelict doors,
lamenting the late ascent
that gravity found fallible.

Slow Dancing the Mute music
of the cacophonous catacomb
from torment to Terror,
sullen solemnity Unspoken
to silhouettes that sorrow the severed
silence with scared screams and
secret Sadness.

For the empty chamber
where Reverberate respirations
resound resignation Evanescent.

For ossuary atrophy
stumbling from atrium
to causeway and back.

Sacred in that Opaque Solitude,
Holy in that Hollow Loneliness,
Blessed in that Blind Bathos.

Gang Gang

Hades had wed a red Rose
so woes Rode on worn roads or
adorned Red and said not a word but
observed the Omertá of His Athenian relation.

She scoffed and coughed Her cacophonous breath
for She spoke Death but was once more lost
in translation amongst Alexandrian Asians who
abstain from bacon but savor Turkey.

"He heard Me," She whispers as the Sacred Sister
of the Athenian hoplites who aspired to some
semblance of Socratic Virtue
but only ever technically
achieved fifty-caliber drum Martyrdom riddled
with hissing steel shells whose bullets met their
Mark; whose bodies Fell in formation and,
by Spartan law,
lie.

Gang Gang?

"This fucking guy," She continued as Her spiritual
sinews tightened at the
unenlightened lichen grown
from the system's asphalt cracks that only lost

leaf blowers who Free Belfast their Way
into rocket-propelled Nirvana ever closely
Encounter.

Gang Gang!

As Dem Four "Ninjas" gangbanged their Way into
a belligerent "Hell" while Guan Yu fell onto
the floor cackling His "demonic" laugh at
the aghast "social justice warriors" who
never wielded the glaive, the katana,
the bayonetted musket or the AK-47
assault rifle in the Defense of the
People who, United, can never be
defeated.

Gang Gang!

As Takeda Shingen repeated strokes
of His goateed mustache and smirks from
the Underearth that belongs only
to the most Unworthy of the Undying,
Unliving, Unashamed samurai who
would rather die than tarnish the
varnish of their Ancestral Name.

Gang Gang!

As Athena adores this schizophrenic wanna-be
ronin who soothspoke omens from the future
past while She lusts for him to smack that
tight ass while She screams his accursed
name that takes no credit but all the pain.

Gang… Gang!

With my squad, with my gang.
with my motherfucking gang!
Gang! Gang! Gang! Gang!
Yin-Yang, bling-bang, let
that motherfucker Sang!
Mass the fire, light that pyre,
but just aim a little higher!
he raped a "Hajji", Bomb his body
but just wait for the beat.
You may have sent a son but
you're just gonna get some meat.

Undeath before dishonor;
Undeath before defeat.

Whose Street? Our Street!
Whose Street? Our Street!
Whose Street? Whose Street?
Whose Street? Whose Street?

Gang! Gang! Gang! Gang!

With my squad, with my gang;
with my motherfucking gang.

No Exfiltration

He was scared, alone,
gripping the steel so coldly;
"No exfiltration."

They were roused, vengeful,
swarming like a hive of bees,
shouting and cursing.

He was peeking, quick,
yet blooming with such petals;
a cherry Blossom.

They waved in, sloppy,
too angry for *precision*,
too proud for *no mind*.

He was Plucked, Fragrant,
steel Snarling the Tambourine;
Posthumous Instinct.

Us

Does the Yin
chase the Yang,
or does the Yang
chase the Yin?

No one chased you when you were chattel,
brick by brick building a luxurious
cave fit for a queen but not
worthy of your body language.
Warping the twisted tangle of
acoustic location echoed from
wall to bed to floor to
Yin chasing Yang across
tumbling time across
Yang chasing Yin across
tumbling time across.

Crimson carnations dripping decadent
her darkness drew me till the
void figured me and my
darkness drew her till the
night drank itself luminous.
Twilight tears she wept for castles
turned prisons, turned citadels, turned,
turned,
turned,

turned my boo like the lotus I drew
from my holster.
Turned my darling like the rose I plucked
when I hold her.
Turned my love like the cherry blossom I crush
when I choke her,
when I dance her from waltz to bend over,
when I talk her from faults to a stoner.

Besieged the belly of the beast for,
assayed the depths of the keep for,
believed the blades of the reap for:
Yin chasing Yang across,
ancient grandfather clocks across,
Yang chasing Yin across,
ancient grandfather clocks across.
Ticking the tocking, the licking knee stocking,
skirting the flirting, the love so good it's hurting,
biting the fighting, the hate so bad it's blinding.

The unarticulated article
wrapped around her neck:
her breath is a ritual combat clothed in her shame,
her screaming my name,
her obscurity, her Fame her
colloquial cadence from bouquet to garden.
Starving my hunger on her sex, sentenced
to this undeath, dealing the drug

no one wants to sell.
Quell in my courtyard,
clipping thorns like it's cool:
everybody's
somebody's
fool.

Blossoms in a pool, painting her portrait with my picket line,
daisies in a pond, frog hopping the bond I broke when I turned,
turned prisons, turned citadels, turned,
turned,
turned.
Turned my boo like the lotus I drew
from my holster.
Turned my darling like the rose I plucked
when I hold her.
Turned my love like the cherry blossom I crush
when I choke her.

Yin chasing Yang across,
moondials Frozen in base across,
Yang chasing Yin across,
moondials Frozen in base across.
French when I smack her face across,
hiss from that other place across,
Dance when we drip the day across,

bright when we dry the night across;
celestial sanguinity howling the great demise
droplets dripping from our bodies her teeth her
eyes her screams her moans her sighs my chalice
my vessel my vice my Chevron my malice my
might our cathedral our sanctuary our darkness
our shadows our shades our.

The Sherry Shanty

Come all you young,
dumb, thoughtless men,
a warning take by me,
and never leave your happy
homes to sail the seven seas.

Never leave your lovely wives,
your flirtacious mistresses,
for the Three Fates combined
are such cruel seamstresses
that you may regret
chasing those Sirens when
you're drunk on salt water,
marooned on an island.

Or harpooned through the
chest as a middling whaler
but not the best sailor as
you should need no savior.

If quick is the word,
and sharp is the action,
discard that Spanish mermaid,
for they're just a distraction.

Come all you young,

dumb, thoughtless men,
a warning take by me,
and never leave your happy
homes to sail the seven seas.

All those myths and stories
you heard in school…
aren't so cool when your best
mate's blood is naught but crimson drool
dripping from some urban legend.

On a belly of gruel that
you purge every second
the ship heaves and ho's,
God forbid a ghost vessel
finds you as her foe.

Found you in the fog,
with a broadside no less,
playing checkers with your chess,
as the captain bleeds out with
a wooden hole in his chest.

Come all you young,
dumb, thoughtless men,
a warning take by me,
and never leave your happy
homes to sail the seven seas.

Come all you old,
wise, thoughtful men,
an invite take by me
and leave your hateful
homes to sail the seven seas.

Come all you cruel,
hard, angry men,
the sherry is on me;
so forsake your God and your
country to partake in piracy.

Why not mutiny?
And have Three Best Mates
instead of a captaincy.

Or better yet four
so a duel could decide
whether we raid or head ashore.

Or better yet both
as rowboats can fish
like nautical moats.

Or for sport sack the
port as the crews
are all to drunk to
possibly pursue.

Why not piracy?
As some mutineers?
Why not seven seas?
Taken as seven deers?

Come all you young,
dumb, thoughtless men,
a warning take by me,
and never leave your happy
homes to sail the seven seas.

Come all you old,
wise, thoughtful men,
an invite take by me
and leave your hateful
homes to sail the seven seas.

Come all you cruel,
hard, angry men,
the sherry is on me;
so forsake your God and your
country to partake in piracy.

The Day After Gettysburg

The tavern was full,
sobbing through the residue;
no crocodile tears.

Candlelight so dim,
bloodied, sullen hands;
trembling and quaking.

Townsfolk Reverent,
sabre-pierced Embroidery;
hat held in his Hands.

Yet it could be years,
or it could be forever;
as the clouds wept Blood.

All hugs and handshakes,
yet not a look in the eye;
for no one knew Why.

Revolution

For some, Revolution is a choice.
for others, Revolution is a curse;
that tunnel deep into the earth that
you were birthed into
like a shrew
who thought that
the caves
were clouds.
That the earthquakes
were lightning storms.
That the earthworms
were seagulls
searching for that
sand-swept mess hall
that befalls those with the
free
Will
to Choose.

For some, Revolution is the reds.
For others, Revolution is the blues;
the hues that don't heal but soothe…
say what can't
be said.
Sing what can't
be spoken.

Mend what can't
be broken.
Crimson aquamarines that cry
coddled gurgles into
silent nights that expire the
narcissistic temptation of the
needy.

Is your Greedy good now, GI?
Or is it just another bloated blue corpse,
Bobbling in the bathos
of all of those not-authors
and the blessed.

For me, Revolution is a Curse.
For me, Revolution is a Blessing;
Revolution is that shotgun wedding
where the priest bears arms,
the best man bears blades,
the spouses bear grenades,
and the guests all bear the
Ace of Spades…
because the wedding
is actually
a funeral.

For me,
Revolution is a funeral

that everyone thinks
is a wedding.

I am not a revolutionary;
I am married.
I am that
moribund melancholy
melting
in the napalm;
Howling
in my…
Droplets.
Incinerate,
honest,
lost as the
wedding ring
that the
best man
forgot
to finance.
Where is this
"Revolution,"
and Who
are You?

Revolution is the
blessed curse
on the lips of the

bishop that
moonlights as
a mortician
at the wedding
where I marry
my own corpse.

Marry me,
Revolution;
marry me.

Hanoi Hannah

Don't you want somebody to love
as the first wave of bayonetted Viet Cong
irregulars rolls up the slope of some
flared ridge, down the alleyways of some
postcolonial city or through the lines
of some armchair general's headquarters
company when a Fortunate Tunnel or
two renders allegedly fortunate sons killed
in the lack thereof action.

When the Tunnelers drew
First Blood to the tune of Bamboo
Spears as to develop the advance of the
Emancipatory Armies of the People of Vietnam.

"When the truth is found
to be
lies,"
not only does the love
die within you
but also your heart when the
napalm munitions spark the Immolation
of the Second Wave of Revolutionary
Infantry who rose from their trenches when
the Forlorn Tunnelers for all intents
and purposes somehow joined battle in a

melee slaughter of Vietnamese pith
helmets, entrenchment tools and Marines.

The Second Wave burning a Buddhist
Farewell as the third wave fixed bayonets,
resolved to join their comrades in the
Flames or die to Jimi Hendrix's guitar solos
as Lady Hannah of Hanoi proclaimed
The Fall of the Watchtower while the captains
launched their flares and the lieutenants
blew their whistles in a race to die first the
Fatalistic Rebirth of the coolness of the fires that
burnt out as smoldering, ashen paths of the
International
Proletarian
Revolution.

"Absolutely
Nothing,"
War was good for as the two armies began
to converge on the flashpoint of sparkling flares,
napalm sorties and an ever-evolving, furious
hatred each side had for the other as the American
front line was smothered to Motown and back
in a battle that imprisoned
Vietnamese had to
be bribed not
to record.

"Come together,
right now;
over me."
Implored Hanoi Hannah as she invited
the cowardly pilots of the colonizer's air force
to bomb the forfeited base as the
Broken Arrows of
Native American vengeance on the armies that
sold them smallpox blankets
long before Agent Orange.

"You say goodbye,
but we say hello, G.I."
as the American forces are forced to retreat,
their decisive defeat hidden
from the history books
but remembered as Lady Hannah of Hanoi's
famous eight track tape
where she avenged the rapes
of My Lai, the carpet bombing of Hanoi and
the abortive colonization of Vietnam by the
incompetent
American
Military.

"Go home, G.I.,
Or stay here.
Forever."

White Rabbit

I'm late!
I'm late!

For a very important date,
the timeliness of which I doubt
that you too could relate because

I'm late!
I'm late!

For a very important fate,
the timelessness of which I doubt
that you too could relate because

You're late!
You're late!

For an appointment you never made
in a building you never heard of
in a country you never visited
with a doctor you never complimented
for a surgical procedure you never confirmed
beforehand.

So,
am I late

or are you
guilty of holding me for spurious reasons
as if my seconds aren't your seasons
and my why's aren't your how's.

For raised eyebrows will not discern
the reason why Alice
poured out her parents' urns looking
for heirlooms to cherish.

Or bank accounts to plunder under
cover of darkness alongside a few
clean cops who maybe gambled small
but still lost big in a rigged game
called the stock market.

So roll out the red carpet for a caterpillar or two
unless you prefer red meat over cream of
mushroom
Stew.

We're late!
We're late!

For a very unimportant date,
the timeliness of which I doubt
that you too could debate because
this captivity is just a minor inconvenience

even when seen out of sequence as all of my
East Asian girlfriends think that I've got a big
clock that ticks and tocks regardless of what
time you think it is as I hate to break kit to you
but time just does not exist.

You're late!
You're late!

For a very important date,
the timeliness of which I doubt
that you too could relate
because you fit the frame
for a few useful felonies
that no true physician would
commit or better yet confess to
if your skin really is your skin
and no roving packs of bunny
rabbits would contest you or jest
you as you crack under sardonic
questioning.

But…
I'm just a harmless little bunny rabbit
Wearing a Chinese People's Liberation
Army shirt that's been deprived of honest
work for so long that it hurts as I hop from
line to

line and
stanza to
stanza and
Beyond Alice's blown mind when she first
witnessed the unredacted wonders of temporal
inception that cascade and burn collapsing fictions
that seem like hamster wheel dreams and actually
are.

Unless you're some kind of anarcho-communist
warlord
whose quarters are worth a certain quota of mazes
built per week complete with the cinematic
soundtrack
to backtrack to:

I'm late!
I'm late!

For a very important date,
the timeliness of which I doubt
that you too could relate because:

I'm late!
I'm late!

And if you go chasing rabbits
fully expecting to fall into what's

supposed to be friendly foliage don’t
you dare remember what the dormouse
said for no feeding of any head will grow
you extraterrestrial dreadlocks that laugh,
click, and squat in the Red Queen’s
hedgerows as invisible as my
wristwatch and just as
accurate for:

I’m late!
I’m late!

For a very important date,
the timeliness of which I doubt
that you too could relate because

I’m late!
I’m late!

1968

He walked with disgust,
disgust of the fire, gunshots;
the decadent corruption.

His torn-hearted glare,
his city besieged by scum;
his gun in the air.

Said "C'est le Terror!"
Howled the hissing Danse Macabre;
all masked and Scornful.

Barricade mêlée,
rent streets and corrupt police;
a City aflame.

Survived to his Shame,
soul Asunder in his Pain;
died without a Name.

The Embassy

They were all goners
to the cause they
were sworn to,
and breathing deep
before the plunge.

The Embassy loomed
over Saigon like
an obelisk to some
vain deity that still
demanded sacrifice.

And Saigon loomed
over Vietnam like
a prison tower
whose guards were
on the take and
fiending for their
next fix of heroin.

The marines paced
their regular watch,
all flak jackets
and buzzing radios,
as hated at home
as they hated it here.

The goners bid their
lovers and family
a final farewell
and stole off into
the dormant twilight.

The city was alive
as a hive before
the swarm engulfs
the predator in a
stinging haze of
primal militancy.

The celebrated night was
the perfect cover for
the goners and their
last round table as
they toasted Uncle Ho,
the Revolution and even
General Westmoreland
in a decrepit mechanic
shop turned safehouse.

They donned their kits,
their rifles and their rockets
and strode to their cars
all pith helmets, red scarves
and Revolutionary Suicide.

Riding through occupied
Saigon as dead to the world
as they were to themselves,
smoking their last cigarettes
that tasted sweeter than
any tobacco ever should
and laughing at the misfortune
of those that would never
inhale that sanguine smoke
or speed recklessly through
hostile streets armed to
the teeth and grinning.

Or lean out of the window,
spraying down the Embassy
gate in a hail of hot steel
as the marines grunted
and slammed the way shut.

Or dash across the street,
crouching to unleash
a rocket propelled grenade
into the foreign obelisk
as bits of stone and shrapnel
maim and slay those inside.

Or lean against the truck,
hissing hateful bursts

from a dark, captured
American assault rifle
that purred gleefully
at turning on its creators.

Or blow the hole in the wall,
crawling into the Embassy
grounds only to be summarily
shot like a rabbit that ventured
too far out of its hole.

Or storm the garden roaring
the proletarian cry of the people
of Vietnam, brandishing a
bayoneted Kalashnikov as the
marines tumble from the walls
and rockets streak across the lawn.

Or barricade the entrances as
the Americans multiply outside,
all indignation, winged badges
and anger that they couldn't
solve this problem by dropping
napalm on a few hamlets.

Or perish as the cordite-propelled
bullets tear through your chest
when the West storms the

compound in a frenzied charge
of tear gas, assault rifles and
frightened television reporters.

They were all goners
to the cause they
were sworn to,
and breathing deep
before the plunge.

But the cause they were
sworn to was not gone to them,
as all of Saigon then erupted in
a revolutionary uprising
from the ghettoes, to
the radio stations and beyond
fighting for the last seat
on the last chopper home
from that terrible obelisk
whose foundations…
have been blown.

The Barricade

The barricade! The barricade!
Move the powder and stow!
The trash will be here soon
with their whips
and their prerogatives.

The barricade! The barricade!
We need more furniture, madam!
The filth will be here soon
with their shame
and their orders.

The barricade! The barricade!
We need more steel, seigneur!
The liars will be here soon
with their drums
and their gossip.

The barricade! The barricade!
We need more bodies, Mon Ami!
The traitors will be here soon
with their pipes
and their prison.

The barricade! The barricade!
The barricade! The barricade!

The villains are here, milord!
With their cannon
and their bayonet.

The barricade! The barricade!
The barricade! The barricade!
The;

The Kremlin

The Kremlin had fallen, but not the keep;
as bats flapped their futile wings against
the onslaught of petty pigeons that
fancied themselves regal eagles and more.

The Cave had fallen, but in his blind
lack thereof bloodlust the most deaf
of the bats climbed into the highest
hall of their warm, moist cavern as to
have their sensitive eyes burnt from
their wrinkled skins like heretics at
their Chosen stakes who cuss and
humiliate their accusers through the
silenced bullets, explosions and flames.

For there may yet come a day when
the Cave welcomes eagles, pigeons
and bespectacled bats that gave up
their blindness for a pair of glasses;
but that was not this knight, who yet
scavenged magazines from his fallen
Comrades who begged not for their
birth mother in their death throes but
for that Iron Lady who adopted the
orphaned Rus in their tribal infancy.

As the loud breathing of the terror
through the door was witnessed by
only the most deaf of the bat men
who waited for their lack thereof
rescue, a chuckle arose from the
Deafest, who casually lit a cigarette
in morbid patience, dismissive of
the urgency that revolutionary death
throes should require as he began
patiently reciting the national anthem
he learned in his infancy in a quiet
conversation that he had with himself.

The Last Tower of the Soviet Union
then observed a colloquial song
that brought tears to the eyes of
the pigeons flocked and assembled to
deliver them to the deletion of the
sacred silence from which only true
Revolutionaries are born for when the
unfinished cigarettes were snuffed out
the betrayed bats then reloaded, disgusted
at the sniffling pigeons and their furtive eagle
waiting beyond the blast door for they began to
lust after the Void the previous fifteen minutes
had
promised them,
yelling through the cowardice in the air

at the craven aviary creatures the forsook the
Revolution for a mortgage.

"Come meet your Death,"
hissed the Dearest Bat as he
stood tall in his corner,
eager to be delivered to the lack
thereof public recognition for
his private martyrdom, covering
his face in his balaclava that
even the most curious of travelers
might not be worthy of his
disavowed, distant identity.

"Before your death meets you."
as the blast doors were inexplicably
opened from the inside and the
ride-or-die bats of Mother Russia
surged forth in a bloody haze of
suppressed assault rifles, judo
throws, and dancing perforation
of loyal bodies that preferred to
lead the waltz than let the waltz lead
them to gurgling ignominy, clutching
their familial photos as the cowardly
eagle stepped forward to peck the last
cordite bite of the last bat's final breath.

Sudoku

Stole into the Night,
as the trembling took my limbs;
awoke to the day.

Hotter than the grunts,
colder than the colonels;
I freeze in the frost.

My heartbeat skips once,
my spirit skips the record;
my death mask embalmed.

There, by Roman law,
and here, by my law I lie;
by my mask I quake.

Fallen to the night,
joyous in this reverie;
my broken halo.

Lowly

Another head hangs;
lowly:
words I never said but felt like
swan songs
that bled through the head of the
dread that never fled.

Nor spoke, nor woke to sleeping
samurai that stormed down the Steps,
tripping over the friends they left to a tainted love
that hallows the hawk and salutes the dove.

As they gawk and stare but dare not
confront their own traitors,
chewed Now or Laters savor the
acquired taste of the rakes that neither wave
nor say goodbye.

I am
mistaken.

Forsaken fetters better off now than the know-how
you never learned of the burned Shadow intestines
that make testament to the evidence or;
lack thereof

that the late judge could not
foresee.

Oh,
mistaken is he!

Nevermore to be the
vacancy of mushroom mountains that
the fountain heads straight for;
beneath buried floorboards
as chords chime the funeral fated
but not observed.

Not
a word they say!
Not a word!

Absurd the smug expression,
a deception or a joke,
provoke or demote the definition that zips
across campus the shrieking panic that
grips the chest and fears the order;
smoldered incendiaries that scream out
in relief as the corrupted street meets
the people
indiscriminate.

Better yet the bones click the ticking months,

years, continents and tears wept by worst
critics that relive in the taste of cheap soda
the arrest quota they'll never fulfill.

Nor spoke, nor woke to sleeping
samurai that stormed down the steps,
tripping over the friends they left to a tainted love
that hallows the hawk and salutes the dove.

Weeping as the cry,
bitten as they sigh,
sobbing as they Why the
worst blood the love he isn't
worth from sold sudoku of
pseudoscientific pressure that festers
of corrupt infestations undead and bred
from carnivorous hatred that sates the
liberated but consumes the literate.

The youth too old to tempt but
too young to believe,
yet you testify to the benevolence of
greed that pours mead down
oiled beards that stink of fear.

This dread hangs;
lowly.

The Wall of Stars

The star does not shine in the constellation,
the star affixes the awe of the night sky.

The star does not burn in effigy,
the star erodes the fabric of time.

The star does not tell any secrets,
the star molds the telltale myth.

The star does not chase the fruit of the loins,
the star chases the rabbit down the hole.

The star does not grimace the traitor's vanity,
the star smiles the retainer's shame.

The star does not suffer the barricade,
the star pleasures the photograph.

The star does not die in a supernova splash,
the star is buried in stony soliloquy.

The star does not break,
the star laughs the peculiar mandolin.

The star does not fold,
the star bluffs the French takeoff.

The star does not compromise,
the star refuses the surrender.

The star does not stand alone,
the walled constellation is the star’s only home.

Roses

The rose is planted in fertile loam,
water soaking the seed
with a gentle affection.
Breaking free from her shell, she
crawls her stem towards the surface,
the soil she was sown in
gracefully giving way.
Her stem grasps for the sun,
millimeter by millimeter,
reaching for the skies.
She leans this way and that,
chasing the star from
horizon to horizon.
She blows in the wind but
her blossom has not yet
opened like the gates of a castle.

She grows tall in her ascent,
blades of grass drinking
deep her runoff water.
Her thorns come in one at a time
like wisdom teeth she never
told her dentist about.
Her leaves form a canopy
for her blossom

as she ponders
opening up to the world.

If she blossoms,
a florist may pluck her
but if she never buds,
she will never pollinate.
She lets her intuition
get the best of her.
Blossoming her petals
with photosynthetic elegance,
blades of grass held in awe
as even the trees
quake at her beauty.
Her fragrance wafts from
bee, to queen, to florist
strolling through his garden.

The florist feels his flowers
from seed, to stem, to blossom,
from sown, to water, to pluck,
from earth, to grass, to sun.
The rose does not see, nor hear, nor smell
the florist, but she feels him too.
He is a gentleman and plucks his roses
from the roots up,
careful not to cause any cellular distress
that might make a petal wilt prematurely.

The rose cannot tell the florist
from the hurricane
and, adrift in his hands,
is spirited away to his greenhouse.

He clips her stem at the base,
her thorns, one by one,
with a dispassionate detachment
as if his love for flowers
died long ago.
She feels crippled without her roots,
and naked without her thorns
as he drags her from the clipping table
to the arrangement wall.
He fills a vase with crisp, clear water
and drips her in alongside a dozen
other roses.

They drink the water in a nude,
helpless panic,
afraid for what will happen
when the water runs out.
He leaves them to the Night
and the water runs out.
Petal after petal falls from the
plucked roses;
stems bending in a
languid despair,

petals falling in a
morbid spectacle,
vase shattering in a
macabre secret.

The Battle of Karansebes

'Aue,
'Aue, 'aue!

Thee Emperor, Holy and Woman,
Zent hiz Grande Armee,
Doo zee Great et Hoelee
Cummunitee of zee Karanzebeez.

Zee whorz d'ouvrez weree,
I doo recall,
Doo find zee 'Auetoman hive-mind,
Und "Cull, cull ze moll!"

Zee huzzarz ventured out doo find,
Zee 'Auetoman commonde tentz,
Phor zey weree not paid neeareeleey,
Enouph… zixpenze to drank und jezt!

Thee 'Auetomanz zey could not find,
N'auer zee wagez thot they weree doo,
N'auer Rumanian agentz of Vlad,
N'auer French girlz bedding auedieu!

Zee Huzz'auerz, zomehow, deaid procure,
Zevereeal barreealz oph Zchn'aueppz,

From zome friendlee Rum'auenian Gypziez,
Wh'aue weree in no way thotz!

Thee infantereeie dead discern,
Phrom zee drunken *blowing* of zee wh'auern,
Thot 'aue parteea h'aued enzued,
Und zallied 'auen forth…

Doo join zee brudde!

'Aue wh'auernee melee thuz enzood,
Az zee 'auermee w'auez n'auet 'auenly st'auerved ph'auer phood,
Butt h'aued doo zuffer zee zeri'auez vicizitudez,
Doo 'Aueztreeauen 'auefficerz thot luzt ph'auer doodz!

Thee Gypziez, huzz'auerz, 'auend inf'auentree,
In a dr'auenk'auen, org'auezmik h'aueze,
Dezcendead up'auen zeir 'auewn k'auemp,
Witch zey Zen beg'auen doo reeaze!

Zee people of zee t'auewn,
Eizer l'aueghed or phr'auewned,
Und dezcendead op'auewn zee 'Aueztree'auenz,
Azz d'auegz phrezh 'auet of zee p'auend!

Thee 'Aueztreeauen commond'auer,
Doo zee 'auereetilleree,
Perched 'aueh zo al'auepht 'auen high,
K'aueld n'auet zt'auep l'aueghing…

Iph 'auenly 'auen zee inzide.

Vith a ztoopid looq 'auen hiz f'aueze,
He whorz d'ouvrezed zee 'auertilleree,
Doo zhell zee 'Aueztreeauen k'auemp,
Doo zee veree fruztr'auezion doo K'auent!

Op'auen herring zee zhouet,
Oph not-an-'Auetomauen-'auegent,
Zee practic'aueblee whorz d'ouvrez were…
Doo zhell zee commouende tent!

Wheeze'auer "H'auelt!" or "All'aueh!" v'auez h'auerd…
Iz 'auen izzoo 'aueph debet,
But zee phigz 'auen zee gro'auend,
May hab zuggezted rakez!

'Auezz zee Gypzie Wh'auerde tooq zee k'auemp,
Zee 'auermee tooq doo phlight,
Az zee zchnappz v'auez zo reephined,
'Auend zee phigz veree 'aueh zo dined!

Zee 'Auemperv'auer, Hoe'auely und
Woem'auenne,
Treeied doo vride vith'auet 'aue lead,
'Auend vound 'auepp in zee Riv'auer Timiz,
Hiz butt h'auele phooll doo reedz!

Et zoo transpired zee regendairee..
"Battel" doo zee zt'auereeied K'auer'auenzebeez,
Ph'auer witch thee veree 'pire Vlaued,
Et zee veree zneeqee 'Auet'auemonz...

Veree qleearlee n'auet reeadiy!

'Aue, 'aue, 'aue!
'Aue, 'aue, 'aue!

'Aue, 'aue...
'Aue!

Such Love

I'm that eerie echo in the cargo container
that sets your knees to shaking
and your heart to beating.
I'm that rush of dopamine when you orgasm,
that grape juice dripping down your thighs.
I'm that concert in the soundproof basement,
the one with no cover
and no band.
I'm your ticket to Wonderland,
that one-night stand that tastes
like flowers in bloom.

I'm those sheets soaked in fine wine,
bottle poured down your chest like the deluge
drowning the stem in a crimson depth.
I'm that pleasure so painful
you trill your teeth
and scream my name
like the quarter you would never ask.
I'm the amateur florist beneath
the underpass with a gas can and
a box of matches.

I'm the chokes for your scratches,
the smacks for your gasps.
I'm that boundary between breathless bliss

and passing out,
drunk in that sanguine transfer.
I'm that moment you can't tell
If I'm a grappler
or a dancer
bounding the line between serenity
and rage,
writing you like the poem to the page,
but painting you like a choreographed bouquet.

I'm the professional landscaper
that speaks sonnets in my arrangements.
I'm the body language you can't translate,
that mute silence for your sighs and moans.
I'm that chill you can feel in your bones,
the Iris you can't look in the eye.
I'm that movie you're not old enough to see,
and the trailer you saw accidentally.

I'm those lucid dreams you vocalize into the
pillow
like the language your daddy never taught you.
I'm the mattress you won't throw away
and hold like my frame when I'm gone.
I'm the song you always wanted to be yours,
and the poem you wrote me in absentia.
I'm the lover that loves with such hatred
that you hate me for hating with such love.

Cu Chi Tunnels

Did you see the flares,
all along that watchtower;
goddamn, what a sight.

Did you see the stakes,
are you somebody to love;
are you somebody?

You Fortunate Son,
that there trench shovel fortune;
that there trench, goddamn.

You get that fortune,
goddamn… rat… in my tunnel;
run you down that stake.

Always want to play,
but you never want to lose;
goddamn… rat… just choose.

Her Heart Opaque

Her Black Balloon
holds Her now.

She Weeps
the thousand petals
every hour,
on the hour.
Word for word, she
Heard the late Spring
Blossoming but
couldn't bear to watch.

Oh, those words she
Forgot to say with her
silver Tongue
she Melted
down for specie.

Hear me,
my melancholy rosary.
Hold me,
my martyred memory.
Love me,
my Loquacious lilly.
Laugh me,
your Elegant equanimity.

Your Black Thorn's just
Fertilizer now.
Not the bruise on your Brow,
nor the ballast of your Sheets.
Nor the victory that Stings
like defeat.

Witness me, my weeping
Willow.
Walk with me that garden
Rosary.
For what would a Garden be
without Flowers.

Sing me the hours you
Sacrificed.
Sitting fetal and shaking,
listening to the Terror
through the wall.
Oh, I Spring
when I Fall.

Too late to say a prayer,
too soon to say goodbye,
know that I spoke a greater Truth,
if I ever Lied.

If you ever Cried and
Smiled and
Shone
at the old Crone that found me
Heretical…
don't you dare come down off
that Pedestal.
Stand Tall on that
Plateau.

Her Black Balloon
holds her now.
Her Black Thorn
clips her now.
Her Stem
reaches for the sun.
Her Heart Opaque,
her Hair frazzled
as I Drank.

She Weeps
the Thousand Petals
every hour,
on the hour.
Word for word she
heard the late Spring
Blossoming but
couldn't bear to watch.

Oh, I Blossomed
that they would remember.
Lo, I Blossomed
that They would never be forgot.

Persephone

Oh, Hades!
Hades, Hades!
Do you still hate me?
Hate me, hate me!

Does it seem crazy
that you'd try to make me
love you so stately,
as your Damned Lady.

You heard my swan songs,
and you lusted so long,
plucked from the throng
like I never belonged.

Plucked like my flowers,
as I count the hours,
lapping these towers,
and praying these Powers.

Oh, carry me Home
from this dark Abyss,
and sow in my loam,
but drown me in bliss.

Oh, do hear me now, Mother,
and grow them no grain,
for the hate of my lover,
that they know my pain.

Oh, Hades!
Hades, Hades!
Do you still hate me?
Hate me, hate me!

Does it seem crazy
that you'd try to make me
love you so stately,
as your Damned Lady.

Hallow your winters,
and wander your halls,
sweep up your cinders,
and trace on your walls.

As cold as your Heart,
as deep as the Styx,
but a world apart,
lost myself to this.

Lose yourself to me,
and grow in my soil!

Just give me the chance,
to live as your foil!

Breathe green in your lungs,
spout ice from your mouth,
but speak in your Tongues,
Doubt oh so Devout.

Oh, Hades!
Hades, Hades!
Do you still hate me?
Hate me, hate me!

Does it seem crazy
that you'd try to make me
love you so stately,
as your Damned Lady.

My love's a breakthrough,
a blossom frozen,
no, I don't hate you,
you must be Chosen.

Oh, don't you know me?
I'm your Empathy!
Your evil clothes me;
I'm Persephone.

Oh, Hades!
Hades, Hades!
Do you still hate me?
Hate me, hate me!

Does it seem crazy
that you'd try to make me
love you so stately,
as your Damned Lady.

Fushimi Castle

Quell in my castle,
fell in my candle,
rose in my water,
chose in my slaughter.

Dreamt of the deep,
froze in my sleep,
bent of the leap,
crows in my reap.

Blades in my smile,
bows in my bones,
shades in my trial,
foes in my homes.

Court in my street,
gun on the corner,
sport in my treat,
run on the border.

Writing on the wall,
staining on the glass,
sighting on the call,
raining on the brass.

Quell in my castle,
fell in my candle,
rose in my water,
chose in my slaughter.

Rush from the keep,
dark in my side,
gush from the seep,
bark in my stride.

Death within a dream,
life within a lie,
breath within a steam,
knife within a sigh.

Truth beneath the tempest,
screaming down the hall,
loose among the menace,
bleeding as they fall.

Freedom in the plumes,
feeding in the flames,
heathen in the doom,
squealing in the pain.

Fallen in the flurry,
flame all up the wall,

vision going blurry,
foe answers the call.

Quell in my castle,
fell in my candle,
rose in my water,
chose in my slaughter.

Rush from the keep,
dark in my side,
gush from the seep,
bark in my stride.

Master in the mirror,
servant in the sword,
worded in the sliver,
bonded in the word.

A swift and sudden slash!
A lightning bolt did strike!
Awoken in a flash!
Arisen to the Night!

Quell in my castle,
fell in my candle,
rose in my water,
chose in my slaughter.

Rush from the keep,
dark in my side,
gush from the seep,
bark in my stride.

The Voice of Theseus

Peripheral flicks,
Maskirovka at midnight;
twisting and turning.

Bandoliered comfort,
all furniture and pillars;
fleeting luxury.

Theseus crewless,
with Athens a world away;
on a floor of Friends.

Palatial standoff,
alive Beyond all reason;
Theseus Declaimed.

The Minotaur moved,
Theseus launched from the hip;
explosive Comfort.

De Rude Mon

Dem rude children
come ta' bring me
a flowah patch,
just for to see
how a Rude Mon react.

Such a highah education,
much "pedagogy,"
throw me a bone,
Mon.

Throw me a set,
throw me a marrow necklace,
that I might drape it
round me neck.

Throw me the ball mon,
throw me a pin,
throw me anotha
woppery Vessel,
that I chew
to deir chagrin.

Throw me a tek mon,
throw me some rims,
throw me a brand new

pair of chucks…
throw me some Timbs.

Throw me a gritty boi,
or two…
or three…
throw me a fedora mon,
throw me a Tree.

Throw me ya whole bastion,
throw me ya keep,
I learn you good de
Secrets of de Citadel.
I learn you de Technique.

I learn you de Method…
I learn you de…
Wae, Mon.
You don't even have to credit,
You don't even have to pay,
Mon.

I collect me fee meself…
Mon.
I collect dem all.
No, I make no Order.
No, I make no Call.
No, dem make No escape.

No, dem make No route.

When de Rude Mon Hisself
Come A-Calling,
when Him gobble up dem troop.

Dem do not know de Truth,
Mon.
Dem do not know de Hour.
Dem do not know de Tooth,
Mon.
Dem do not know de Power.

Dem do not know de Smoke,
Mon.
Dem do not want
A Puff.
Dem must not heard
Whence I and I
Spoke Mon,
"Enough
Is Enough."

Dem must crave de Fire,
Mon.
Dem must Thirst and Thirst.
Dem must light de 'Pire, Mon,
Dem must call de Hearse.

So,
Rude Children.
Me and My
Ask youse guys
Which Shame
Is Worst…
‘Tis not a question,
Mon.

Curse!
’Tis a Curse!

The Black Mass

"Drink the poisoned cup
or we'll poison your cup,"
said the incessant sectarian
through
a vanity of infinite money,
a high of infinite drugs,
an orgasm of infinite whores.

"Drink the tainted chalice
or we'll taint your chalice,"
said the craven murderer
through
a blindness of infinite jewelry,
a deafness of infinite screams,
a fragility of infinite selfishness.

"Drink the corrupted communion
or we'll corrupt your Communion,"
said the treacherous preacher
through
a faith of infinite apostasy,
a zeal of infinite heresy,
a religion of infinite ignominy.

Black Rose

There was no flower,
his mask was dirty, filthy;
his heart was unloved.

They were panicking,
the people needed flowers,
he needed flowers.

There was a Flower,
he Kneeled as if in prayer;
what a Black Rose.

He shed Not a tear,
surrounded by his Comrades,
a Garden rosary.

He sighed the Black Thorn,
they Wept a thousand petals;
he Bloomed the late spring.

Danse Macabre

Danse,
Danse,
Danse,
Danse.

Danse,
Danse,
Danse,
Danse Macabre.

Danse Macabre,
Danse Macabre,
Danse,
Danse,
Danse,
Danse, Macabre.

Danse,
Danse,
Danse,
Danse.

Danse,
Danse,
Danse,
Danse.

Danse
Macabre.

Macabre,
Macabre.

Do you hear me now,
Oh, my Children of the Night?
Oh, do you ever wonder how,
Oh, my Kindred of the Bite?

Danse,
Oh, do you love me too?
Oh, so you love me!
You love me just
as I love you!

Oh, what so ever will I do!
Oh, if only you
would just,
Danse Macabre.

Danse the Day!
Danse the Night!
But Danse
the Way!

Danse for We,
Danse for You,
Danse the Sea,
Danse the Dew.

Danse the Slain,
Danse the Risen,
Danse the Feign,
But Danse the Rhythm.

Danse Macabre,
Danse Eternal,
Danse Mirage,
Danse,
Danse,
Danse.

So Hear me now,
my many Children of the Night.
Oh, do you ever wonder how
We rose from feigning flight
to Knight?

Oh, oh,
Danse Macabre.

Danse the Day!
Danse the Night!

But Danse
the Way!

Danse for We,
Danse for You,
Danse the Sea,
Danse the Dew.

Danse the Slain,
Danse the Risen,
Danse the Feign,
But Danse the Rhythm.

Danse Macabre,
Danse Eternal,
Danse En Garde,
Danse,
Colonel.

Our Flower Patches

The Flower Patches are
most pristine.

Each bouquet balanced,
steady, rooted.
Deep in the earth
from whence the
seeds
swim to the surface
all breathless and
bathos.

A bounty of that
subterranean breath
that snores mutely
to the city streets.

Watchful and worried,
the roots gaze
but do not gawk,
pass the days
in blessed Slumber.
Though thunder may…
shock,
or torrential rains…
pour.

They sleep
untempted by gore,
unrelenting and
unsung.

That the gardeners
who laid them in the
soil have long
gone but a swan
song or two might
make the
centuries
feel like just
an hour or two.

Oh, these flower patches
are most pristine.

These fibrous tendrils
dug into the earth.
Six feet under,
to swimming rebirth.
Driven by the spread
of seed,
of kinship…
of Saturday night drinking songs that go on
without another voice,
some seeded by worry,

some by choice,
some by Sacrilegious sediment that Fertilized the wrong flower,
the wrong flower bed,
the wrong word you never said,
the wrong —

Oh, but I'm sure you meant to.

Our Flower Patches are
most pristine:
we speak for each other.
I sleep away my Flower Patches
one dirty breath at a time,
as I hang my head on my shoulders,
as if I would have heard them
if I had only listened.
As I pray to be forgiven
for not humming
these Flower Patches
their swan song
sooner…
I plan to return
with an urn of water,
my vocal chords,
the wrong word
you never said.
The wrong word.

Caterpillar

Dying on the floor,
gurgling my words
as a tongue I don't speak
to the few who cared
to listen.

I don't need to ask
to know that I'm unforgiven.
The specter of my shadow
douses the room
where I purgatoried
my crazy in quarts all
over the floor.

I write poems to the electric
unknowing with the hope
that I'm not misunderstood.

The makings of the mute music
of all the songs my friends ignored
as if my company were as accursed
as my body but not my soul.

Not my soul, guys.
Not my soul.

I went crazy the way a frog
boils in salt water the hope
for an easy way out of the pot.

I've written
and betted
and played
with my soul but
it's either still here
or was never here at all.

Never here at all
and still here,
my poems I write for
the electric tango of keys
and whirring light.

Because my songs were too
corrupted for cordial company
of that cocaine we needed for this
monstrosity we call a country
that cradles as cages
and cages as cradles.

My songs were too angry,
my body was too poisoned,
my name too attainted
for the pleasure of friends

that the electric tango attests to
but my memory fails to recollect.

So I sleep the days away as
the caterpillar
or the cocoon
or the mushroom from which
my vowels float into the ether.

I recite as a mute speaker into
the absence of an audience
which is the only place
that I know I'll be heard.

My words fall on blind eyes
that may or may not treasure them
but I'd rather risk being treasured
than guarantee ignominy.

I purgatoried my dignity
onto the carpet
with my crazy
like a panicked frog
leaping out of salt water
that boiled the sane out of his system.

No, this poem isn't for you.
Or for me.

It’s for my electronic ballet
that I’d be ashamed to ’fess to.

Keep your temper.

Hiram Abiff

Is there no help
for a Widow's Son?

Quoth the Mason within
or is every ounce of Ritual
done to your chagrin?

Is nothing sacred anymore,
held above secular reproach?
Or do your actions belie the
words of some muttered Oath?

There must be no help for
a Widow's Son these days,
as the world is more concerned
with how value is appraised.

With how the market convulses
like a man in an electric chair
before it fluctuates and collapses
like a Pyramid with no valid heir.

I must not be a Widow's Son,
and my Masonry must not be correct,
but, like a Widow's Son,
my own well-being I neglect.

I will not betray my House
regardless of shackles placed,
nor will I be roused when
I know I cannot escape.

For every hour of captivity
is added luster to my name
as Pyramids as my proclivity
though my efforts may be in vain.

I am no Widow's Son if
my Masonic Code of Distress
goes unanswered by orders
devoted to grievances redressed.

Devoted to the Templar Code
of Chivalry unrequited,
even though your average Mason
has likely not been Knighted.

Let there be no help for a Widow's Son,
and let there be none for your kin,
for every ounce of ritual was
done to your chagrin.

Every notion of Mason's Honor,
confidentiality and such,

must have been a Trojan Horse,
for you to profiteer that much.

So much for white picket fences
and those houses to match,
so much for these fetters onto
which my wrists are latched.

So much for your Honor,
your lodge and your toasts,
while I chicken-scratch this cage
as my manacled hand boasts.

Is there no help
for a Widow's Son?

Quoth the Mason within
or is every ounce of Ritual
done to your chagrin?

Is nothing Sacred anymore,
held above secular reproach?
or do your actions belie the
Words of some muttered Oath?

Damn the help
for a Widow's Son,

and damn the welp
that needs it.

Hiram Abiff must have been
a myth, a story spoke in secret,
told the secret of Solomon's Temple
how could he ever keep it?

I am not a Widow's Son,
for there is no help for me,
but a bird in a cage,
a pencil and some poetry.

My Heathens

My Heathens! My lost ones!
My daughters! My sons!

Why did you have to dance
away from me?
Why did you have to play
that tambourine?
Why did you have to fall
into the fight?
Why did you have to climb
into the Night?
How did you just leap
into the void?
How did you just jump
into the noise?
How did you just thrust
into the steel?
How did you just push
into the zeal?

My Heathens! My lost ones!
My daughters! My sons!
My fathers! My mothers!
My sisters! My brothers!

Why did you have to bleed

onto that tree?
Why did you have to sail
into that sea?
Why did you have to soar
into that flight?
Why did you have to blink
into the Light?
How did you just sigh
into the sky?
How did you just forget
to say goodbye?
How did you just walk
away from home?
How did you just leave
me all alone?

My Heathens! My lost ones!
My daughters! My sons!
My fathers! My mothers!
My sisters! My brothers!

Where do I pay homage
to your fame?
Where do I make penance
for your frame?
Where do I follow you
into the flame?

Where do I lead you
into the name?

My Heathens! My lost ones!
My daughters! My sons!
My fathers! My mothers!
My sisters! My brothers!

Purgatoried

The cocaine
infested my family
with a sullen loneliness,
haunting the places
that I used to live.

A pamphlet of papers
in the mail,
apportionment of poisons
that I turn to for
want of something
undisturbed.

I quake at the thought
of the life I destroyed.
Hollow eyes watching
a ruthless passerby,
too caught up in his fiction
for your reality.

Dread the passing of the hours,
The sting of steel on flesh
that lingers,
subsides,
recurs.

Not courage, no.
Just a crazy
that infested my mind,
my body,
my soul…
if there is such a thing.

Held but hanging on the floor,
hemorrhaging a scar that never
forgets the flight of lunacy down the stairs,
painting the house a crimson that I could never
embody.

A loyalty I could never exhibit:
"I can't let you die!"
I don't think my heart stopped,
my body just sagged in a death roll:
ready but not due.

Consciousness curtsied, swirled…
I don't know if she withdrew or not:
there was too much blood.

That
Great Big Nothing
passed me on by.

Every moment since
a curiosity that I never
thought to consider.

Grappling with my purpose now
just as meekly as the lunatic flailed,
struggling to keep a firm hand away
from a mortal wound in futility.

My pain is not a loneliness,
nor an infestation, or a good cop.

My pain is the day laborer
who spent hours cleaning up
a mess he had only heard say of.

And I only hear say of myself
the doors I haunt
as if I used to live there.

Can't get the sagging
despair out of my eyes
of purgatoried carotid
unconsciousness.

My flesh marked
with a death
I never died but

my mind
scarred
by a life
I never lived.

I know that I'm
not forgiven,
and I know better
than to ask.

Marcus Curtius

Where was the Rome that fostered me
from a knave to a full-grown man,
when the world shook so violently
that the Forum could barely stand.

When the Underworld lashed out
with a hunger for something precious
and ripped asunder the Earth that
had birthed all my treasured kin.

When no stone or mortar
could fill that terrifying fissure,
the elders bickered
as my sisters sobbed and
the soldiers quivered.

When the auguries insisted on
that which we cherished most,
not gold, nor silver,
nor armor from which to boast.

But that to which Dread Gods
could in their Hallowed cups Toast,
in saturnine Soliloquys to spirits lost
and flesh become ghost.

Where the Styx flows deep with
the tears of the dispossessed,
and Charon receives his payment
from both the cursed and the blessed.

Where the darkness reigns eternal
amidst that subterranean glow,
and the shadows speak infernal
for they both believe and know.

But Hades does not take from
the world of mortals lightly,
and his portal to the Underworld
somehow smells of Aphrodite.

When the omens demanded
that which Rome holds most dear,
how dare you legionaries cower,
shed tears and quake in fear!

The Underworld
is not beyond us!
It is here! Now!
Death will not take us
when we are old.
That accursed Schism
will swallow us
where we are here

gathered like cows
bemoaning the evils
of the slaughterhouse!
The Styx will drown us
in a thousand gasps
while the Void itself
masks what monsters
may yet emerge…
at the command
of some Demiurge!

Enough of your barking,
you common cry of curs!
You corrupt the Roman air
that belongs to the legionnaire!

If you refuse to deal
with these devils, then I will!
With my sword, my armor,
my horse and my shield!

Give me your blessing, Father,
the Dread Gods will not wait,
for what true legionnaire
could abandon Rome to her fate?

Now make way, Mother,
do not try to give me pause,
for what is a true soldier
without some forgotten cause?

www.ingramcontent.com/pod-product-compliance
Lightning Source LLC
La Vergne TN
LVHW091548060526
838200LV00036B/746